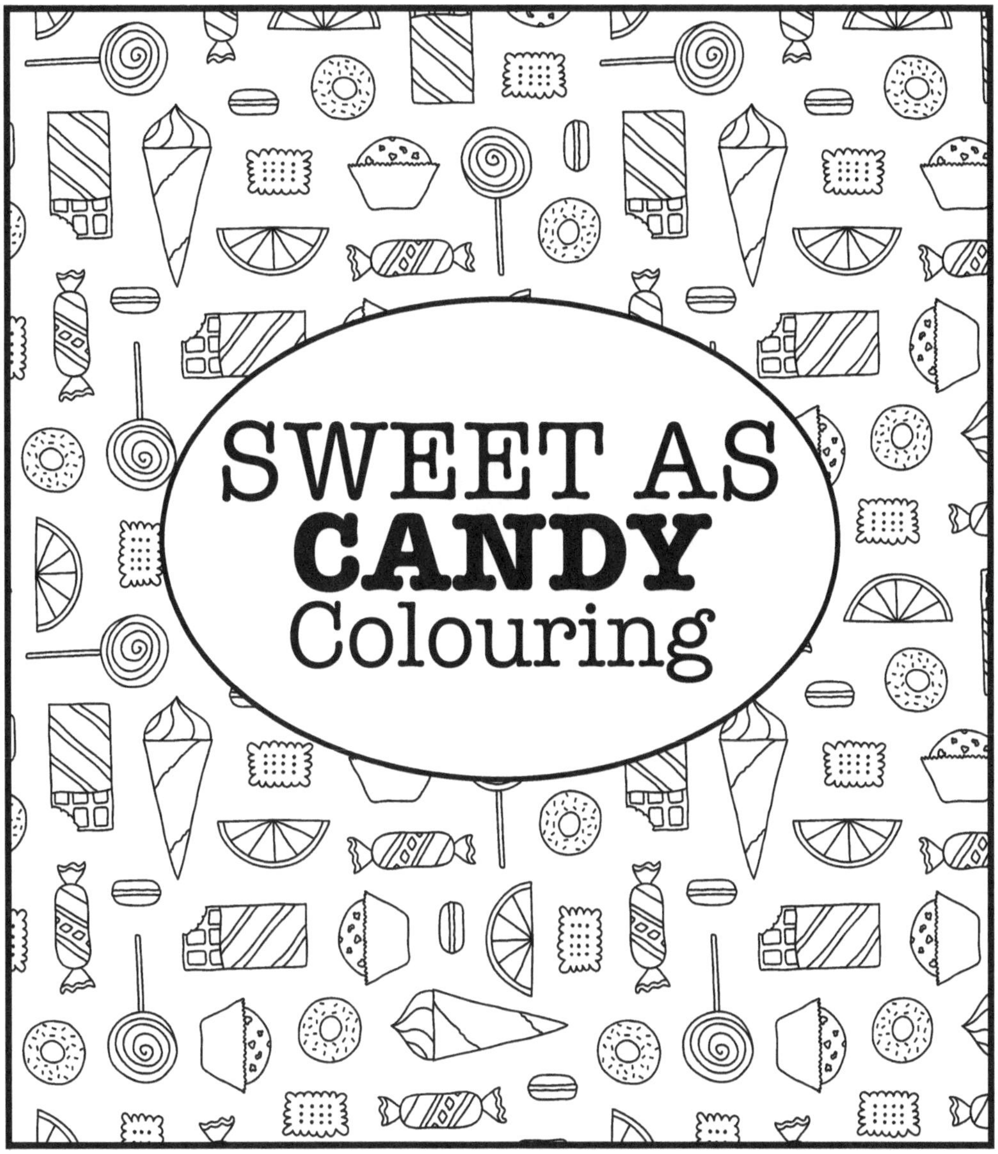

# SWEET AS **CANDY** Colouring

Gorgeous Colouring For Girls **Book 8**

First published in 2016 by Kyle Craig Publishing



Editor: Alison McNicol

Design: Elizabeth James, Julie Anson, Alison McNicol, Shutterstock, Inc.

ISBN: 978-1-78595-125-1

A CIP record for this book is available from the British Library.

A Kyle Craig Publication

www.kyle-craig.com

Love
Love
Love
Love

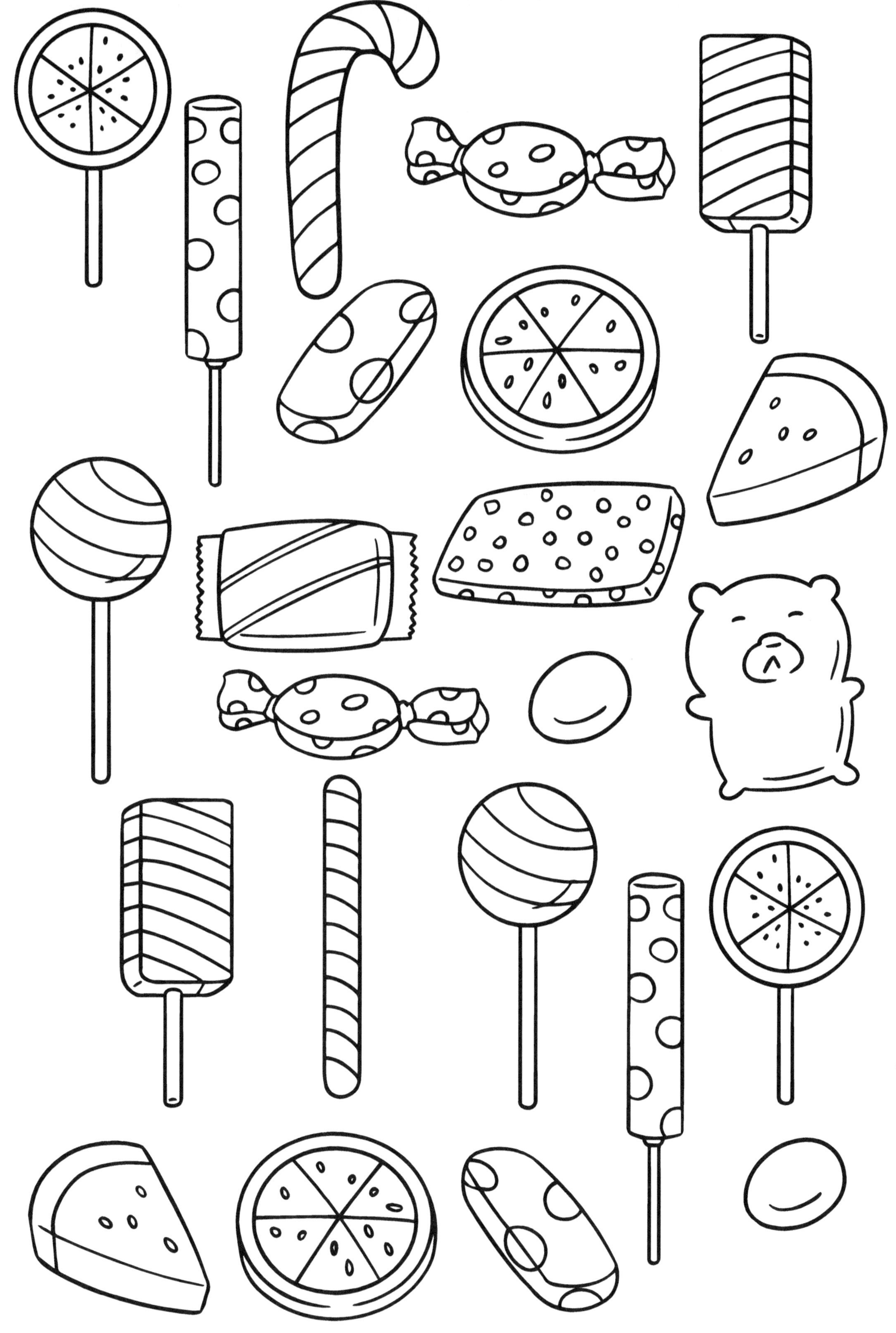

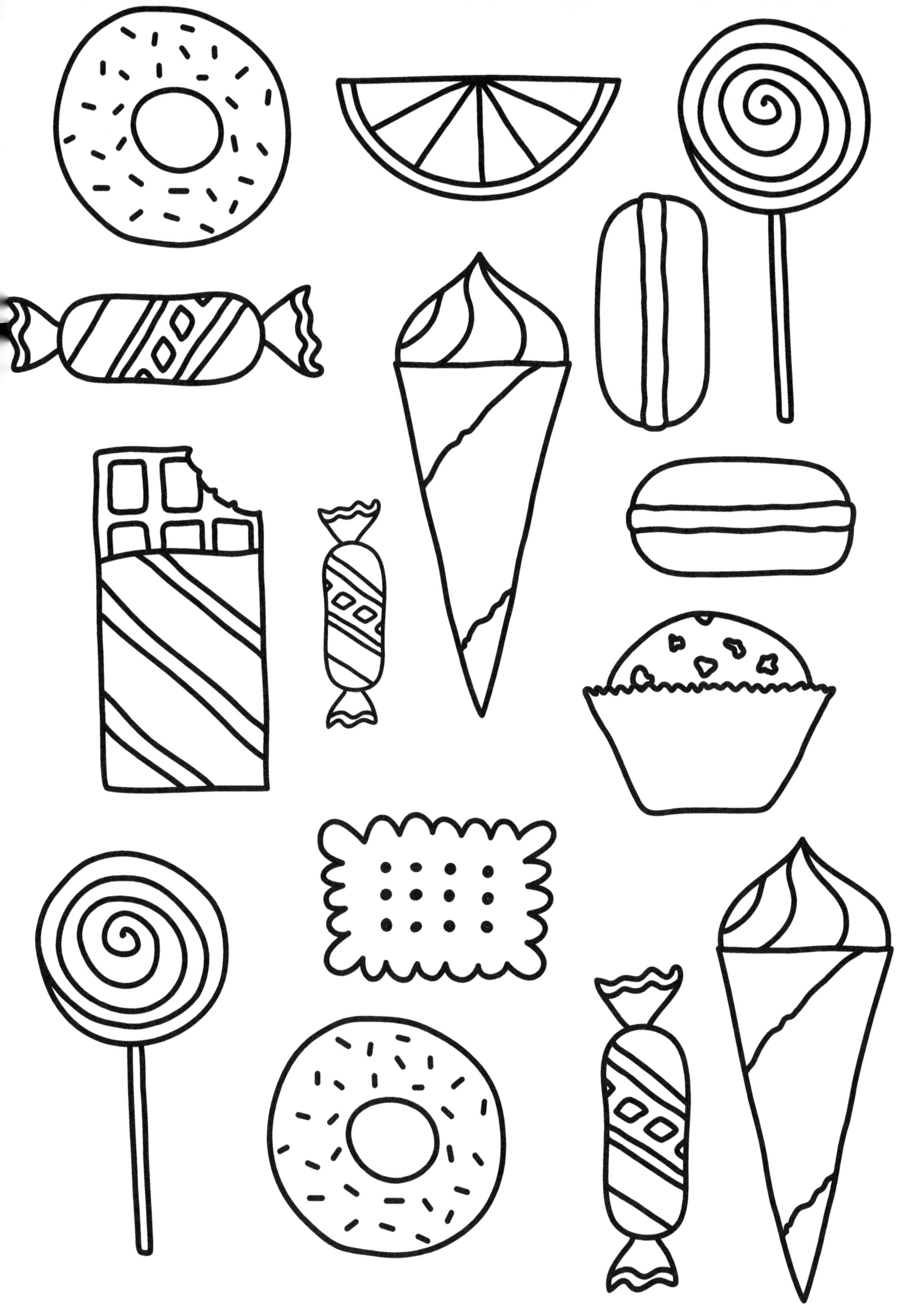

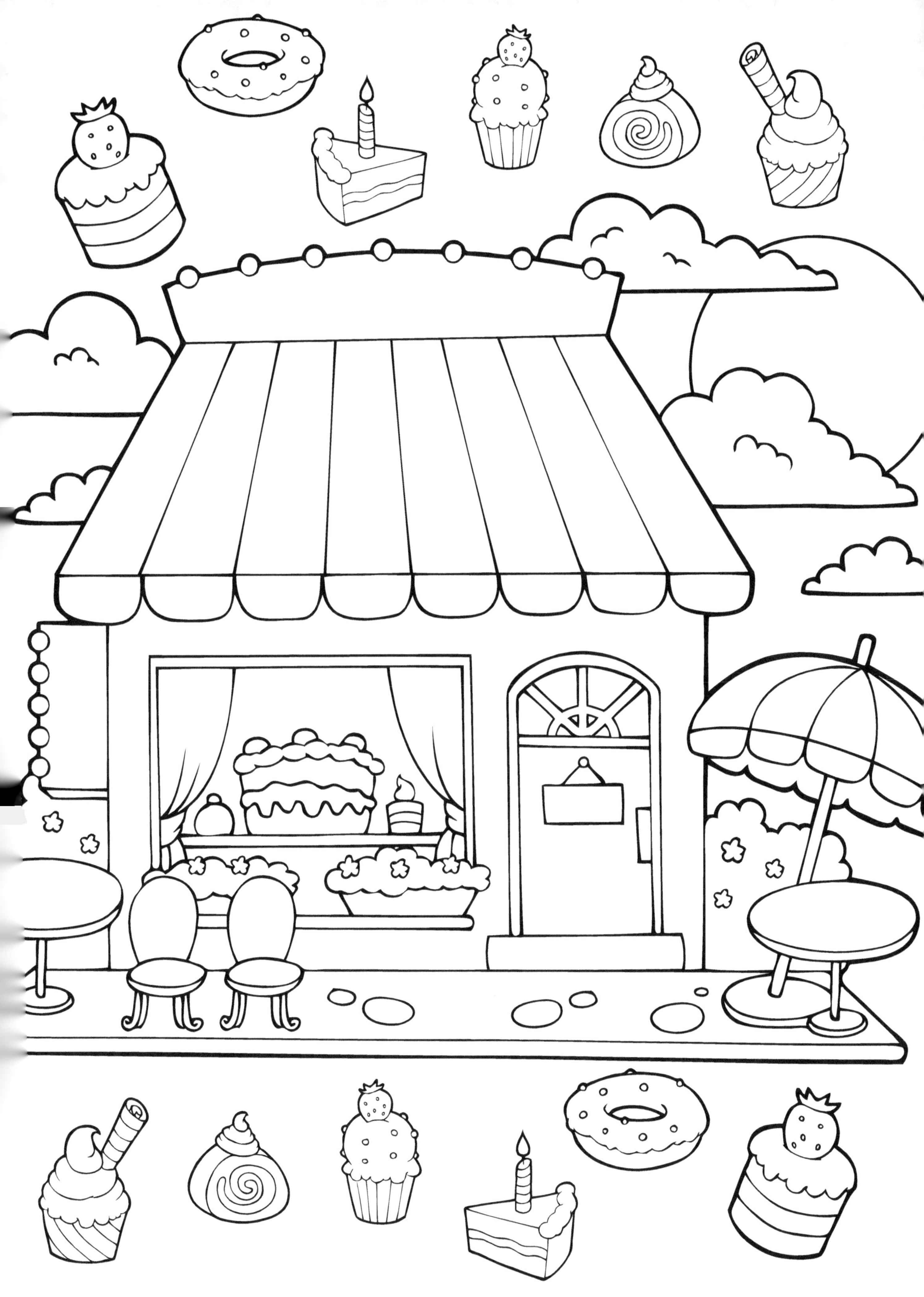

LOVE

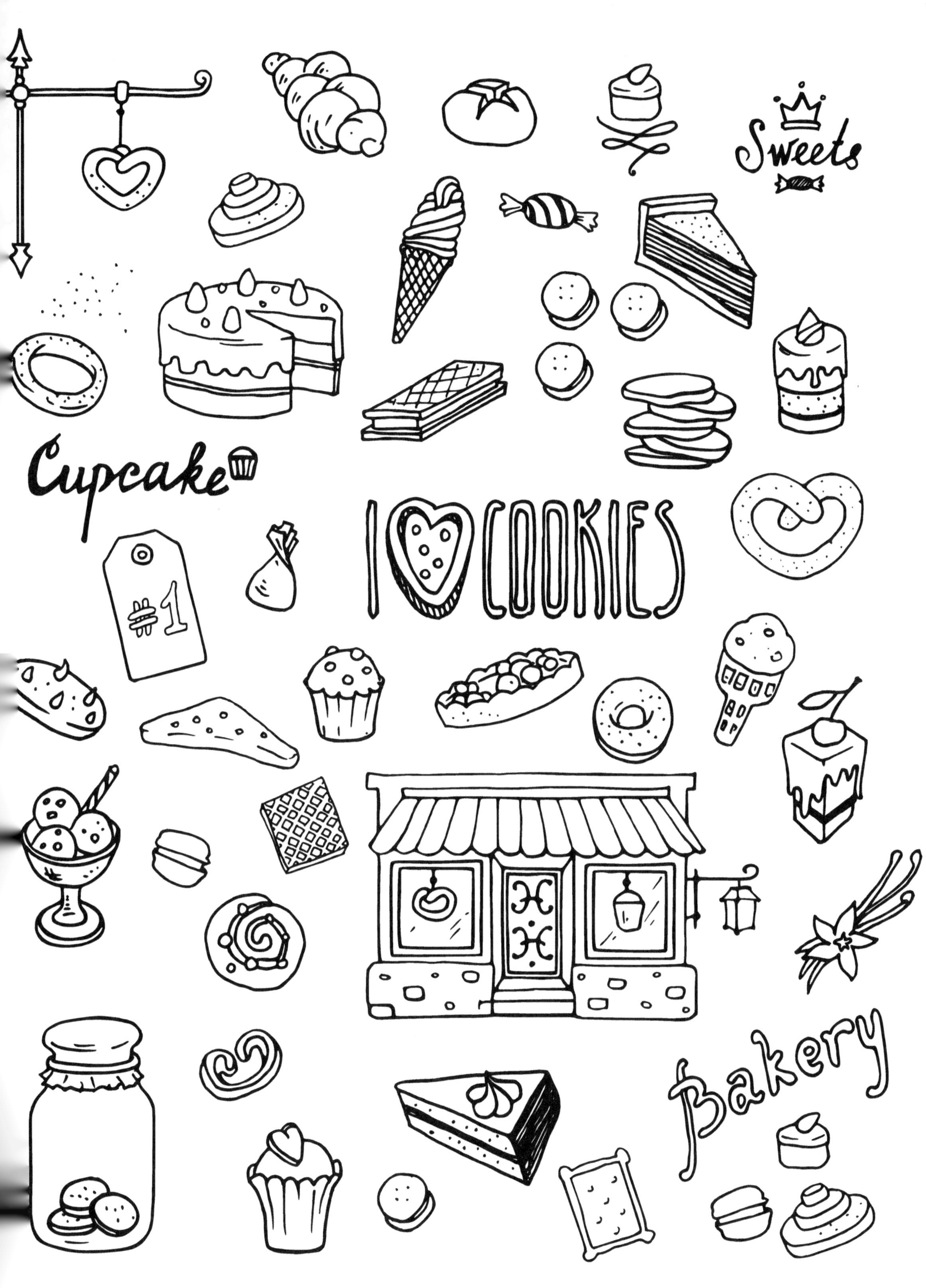
Sweets
Cupcake
I COOKIES
#1
Bakery

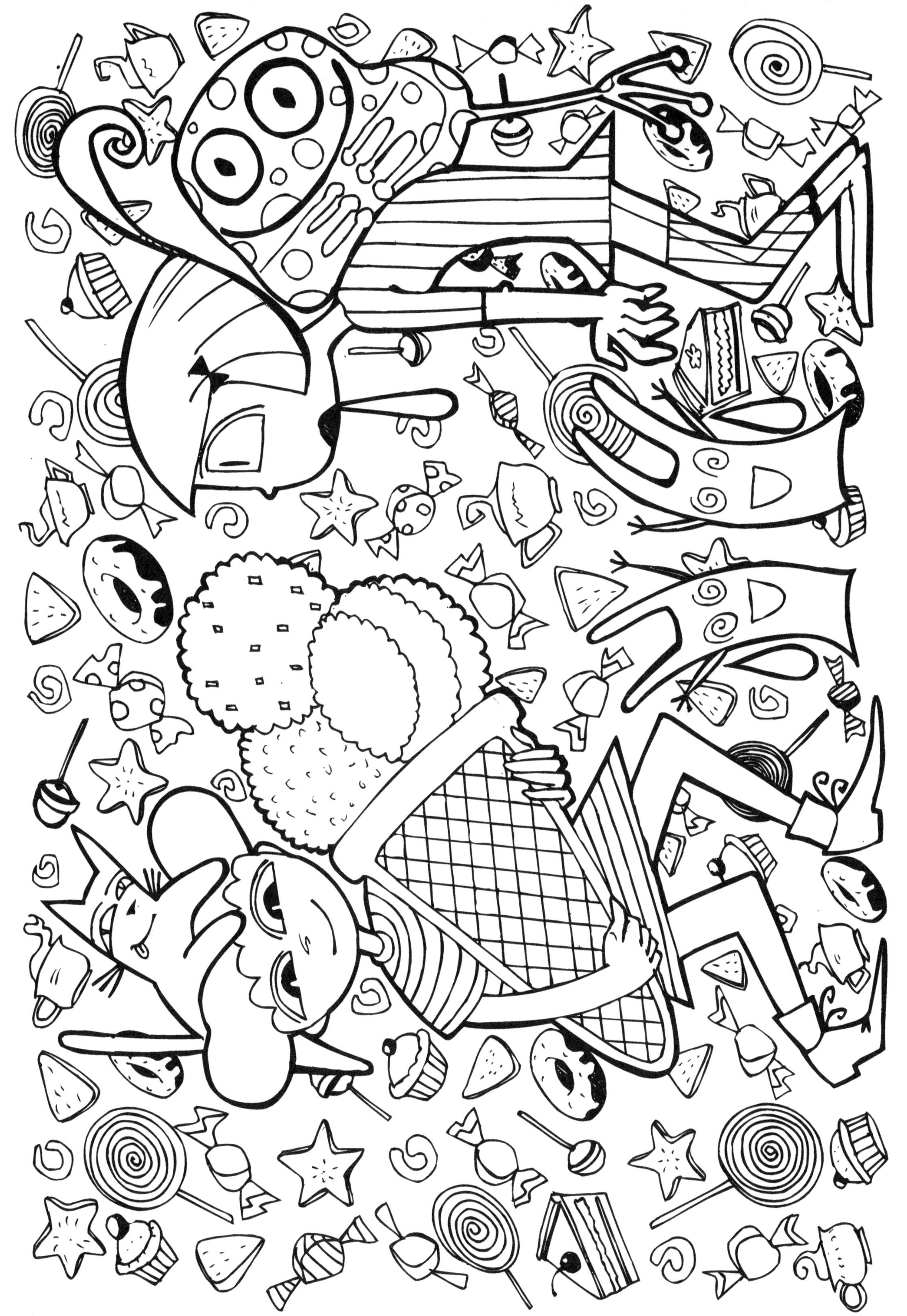

Mousse
Choco
mission
chocolate
Choco Heart
Mousse
Choco
mission
chocolate
Choco Heart

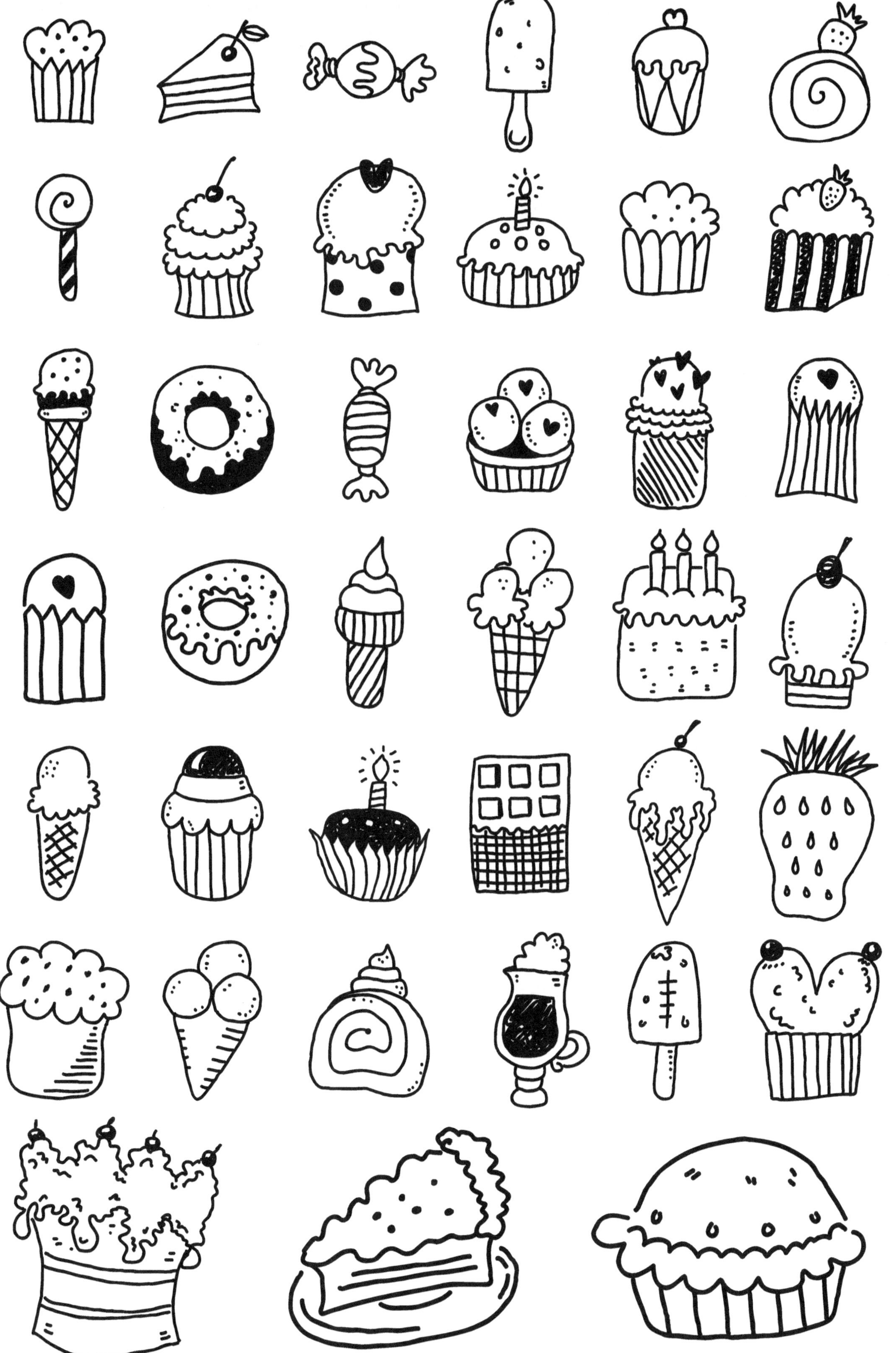

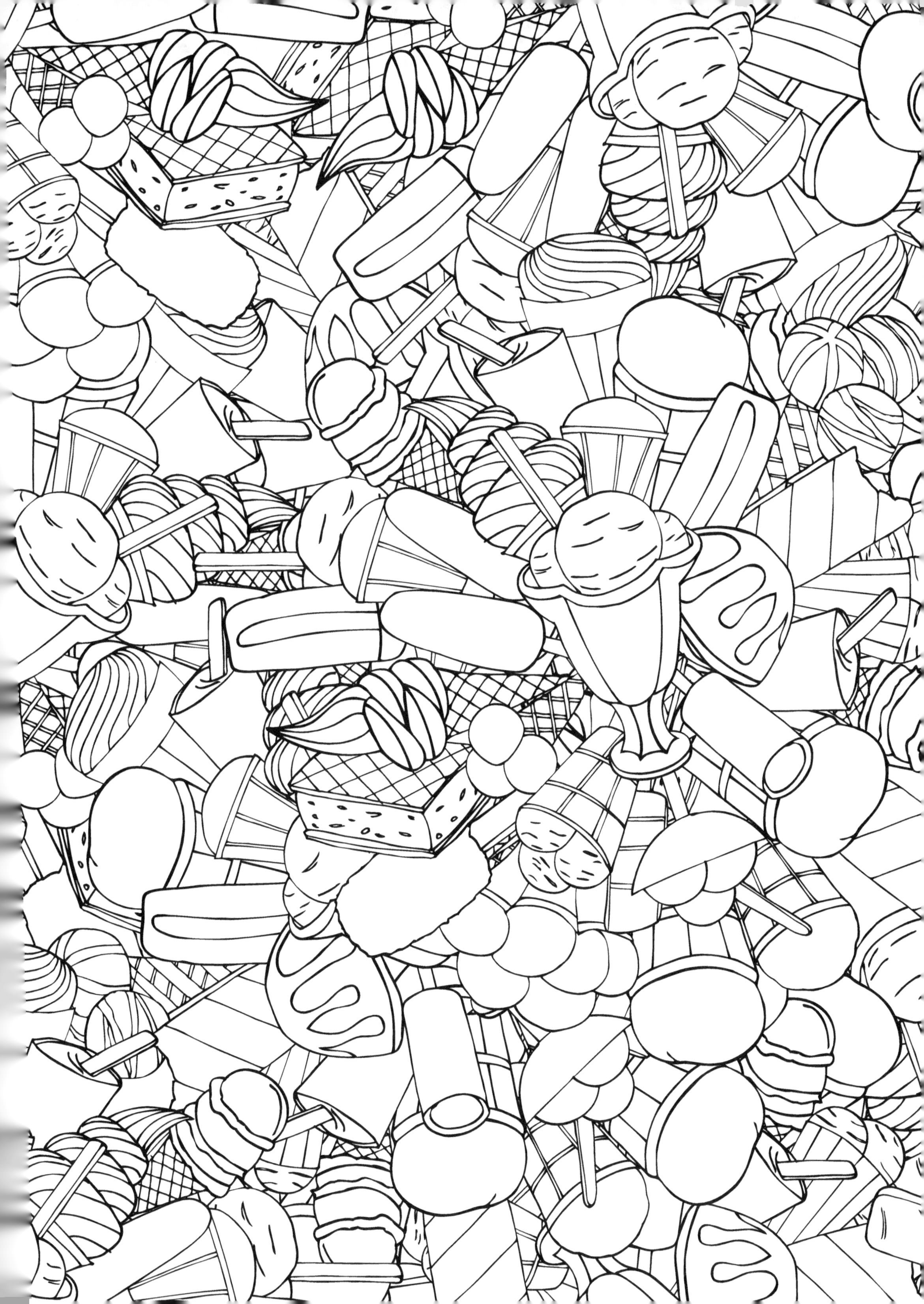

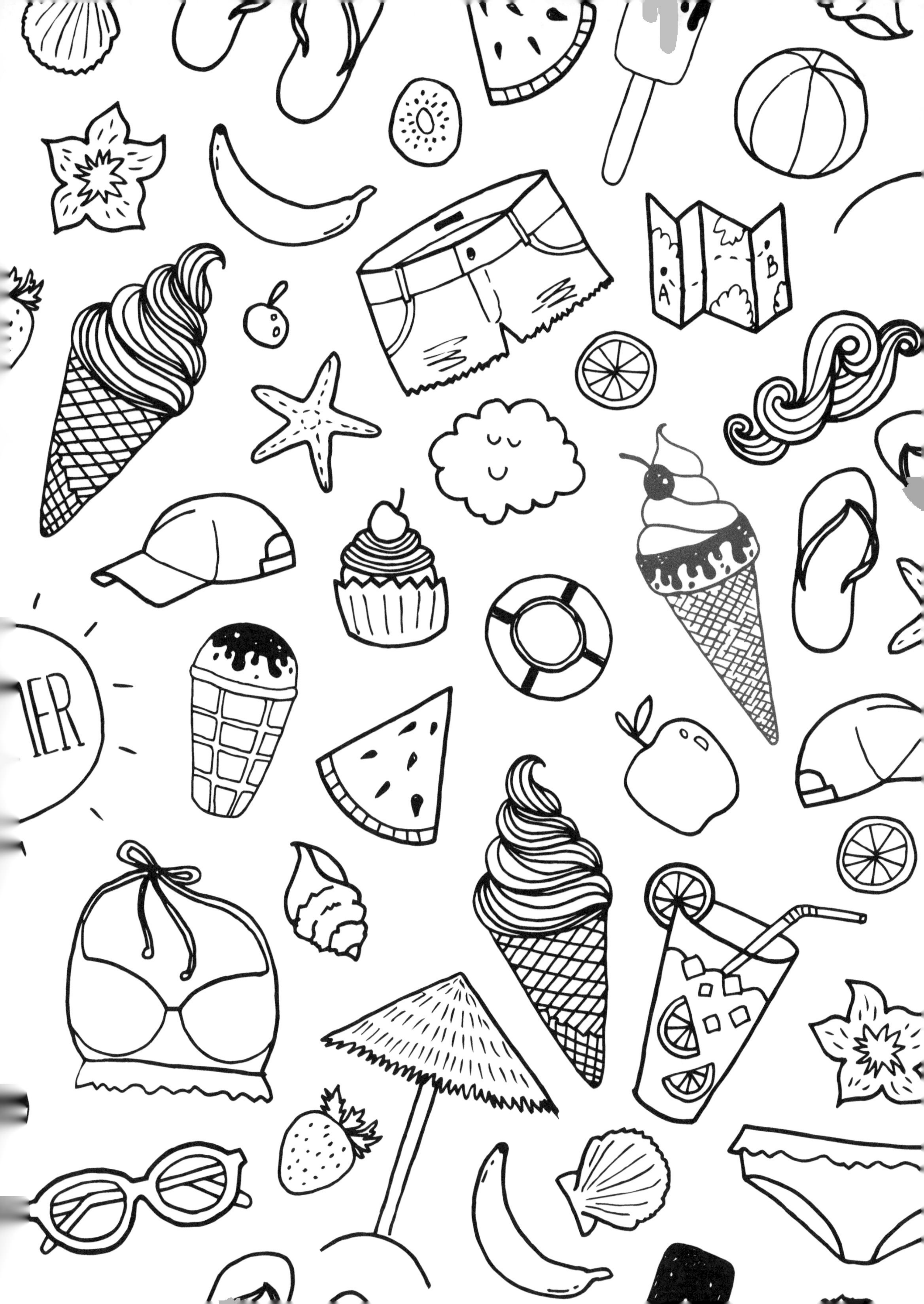
A
B

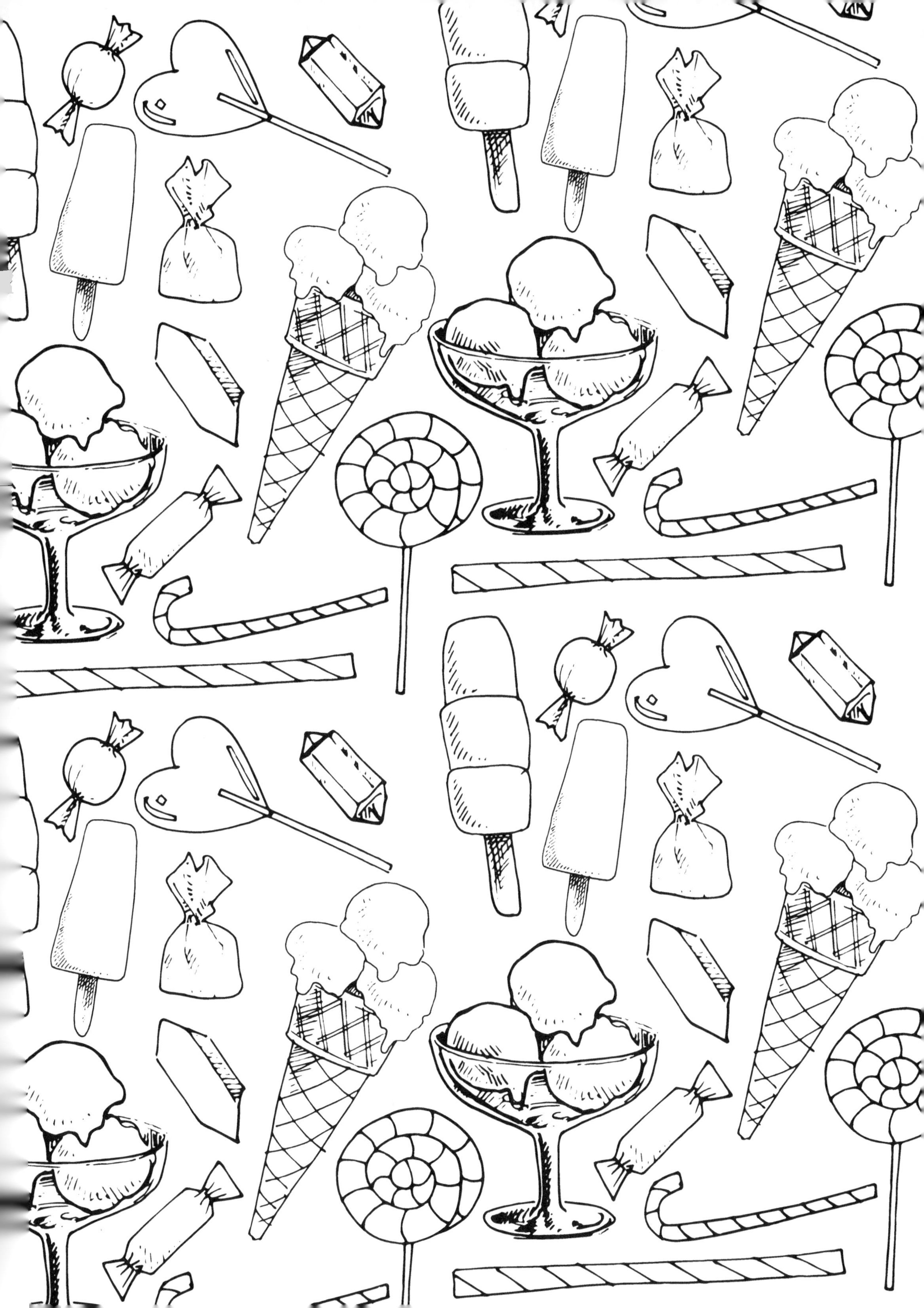

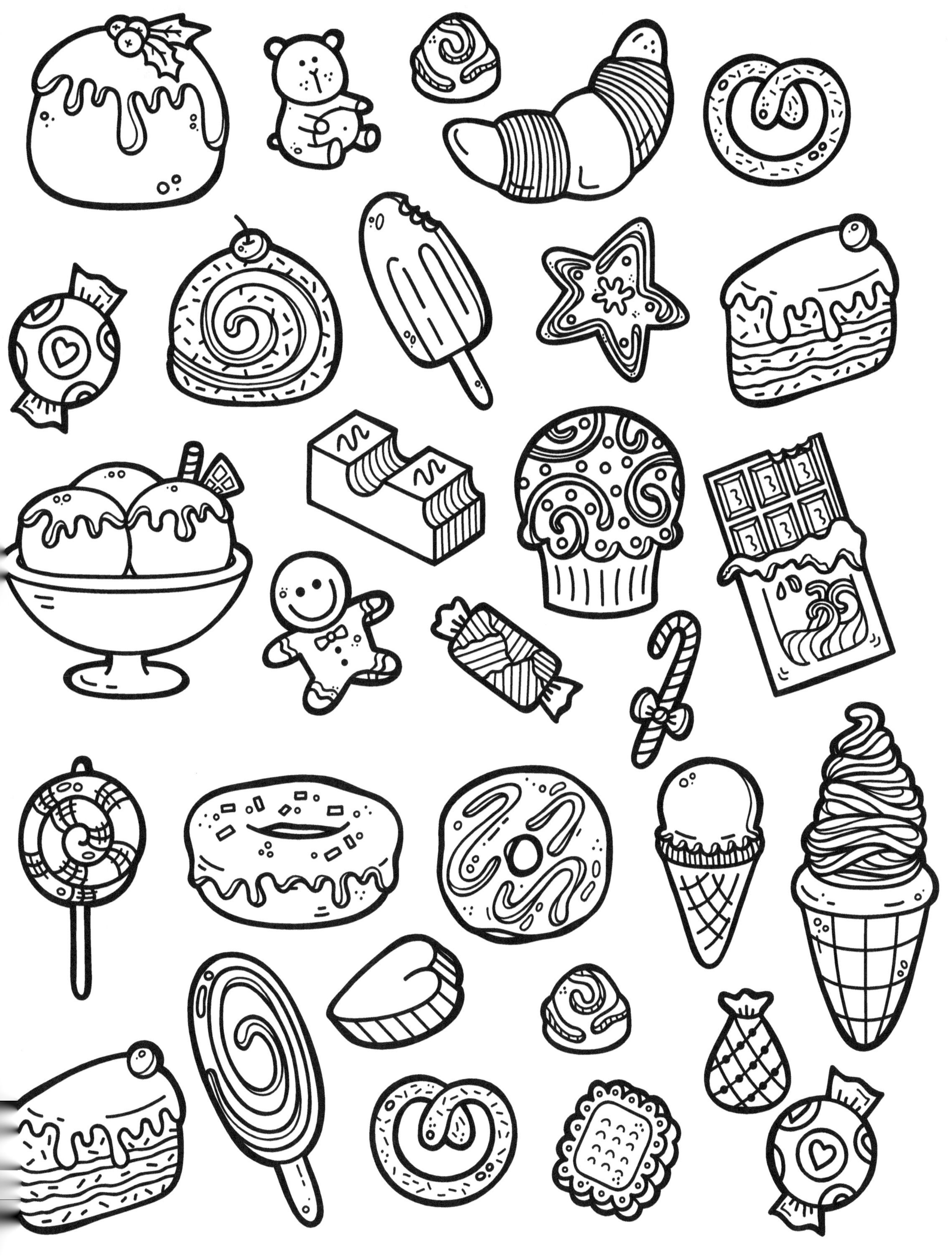

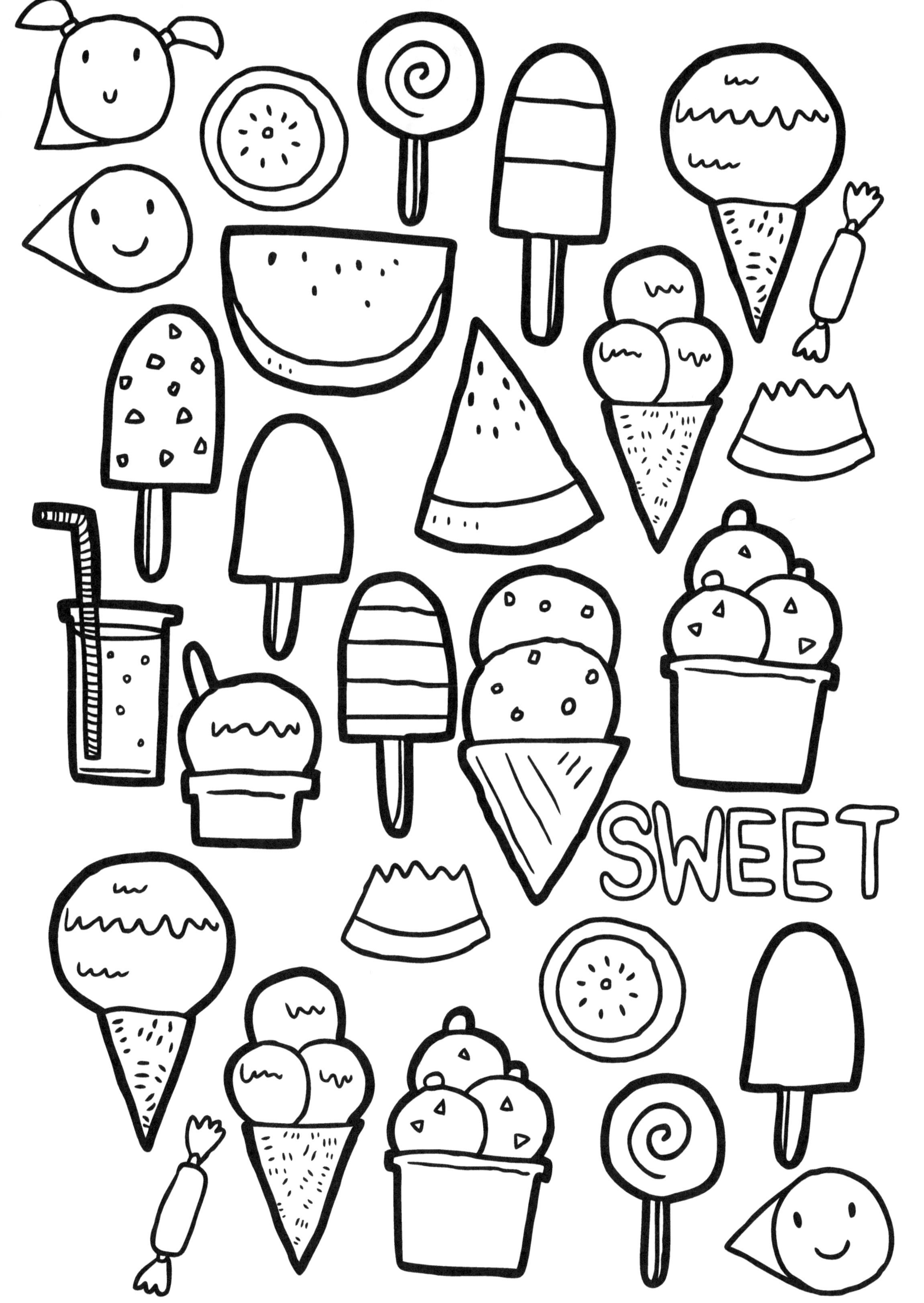
SWEET

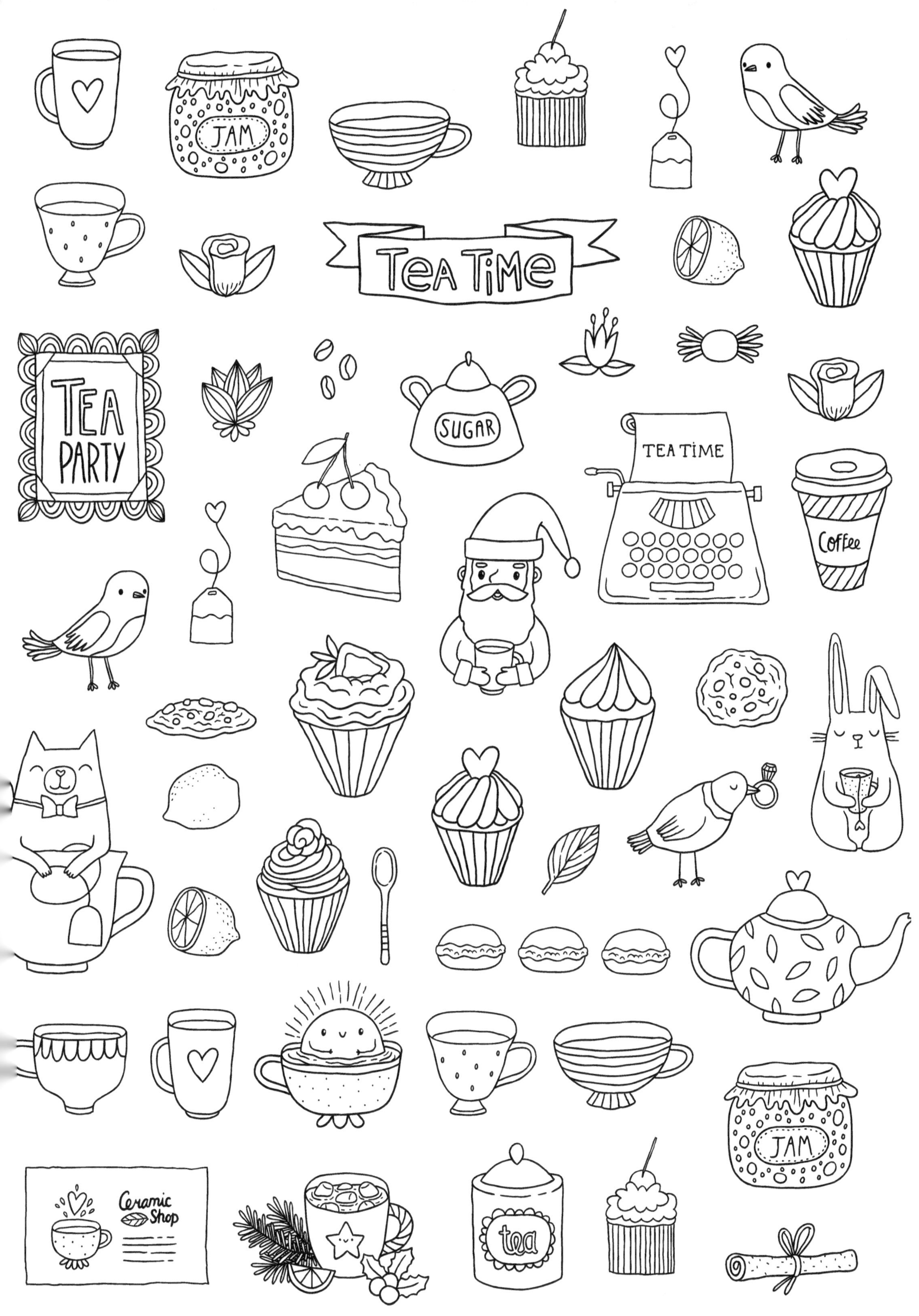
JAM
Tea Time
TEA PARTY
SUGAR
TEA TIME
Coffee
JAM
Ceramic Shop
tea

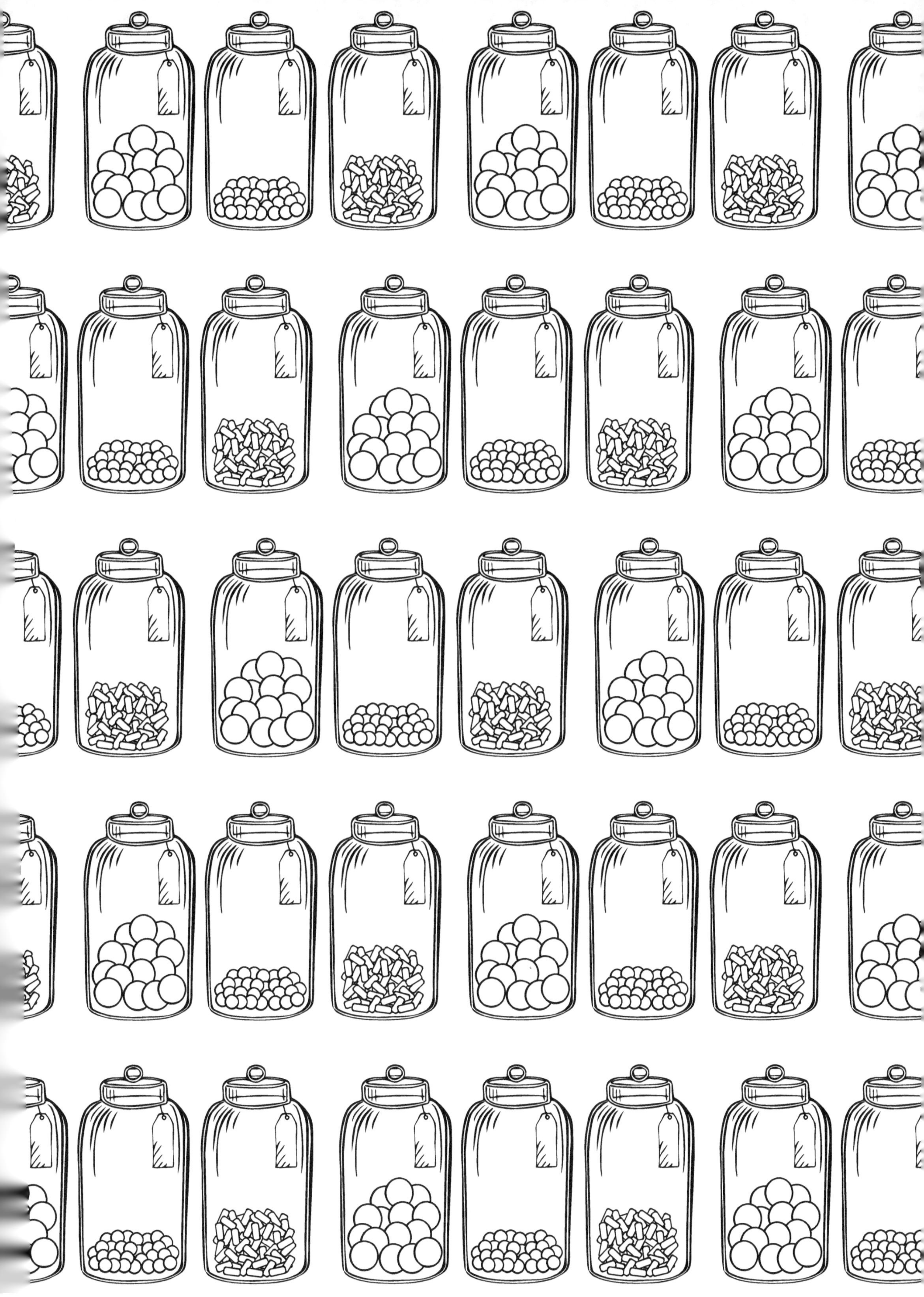

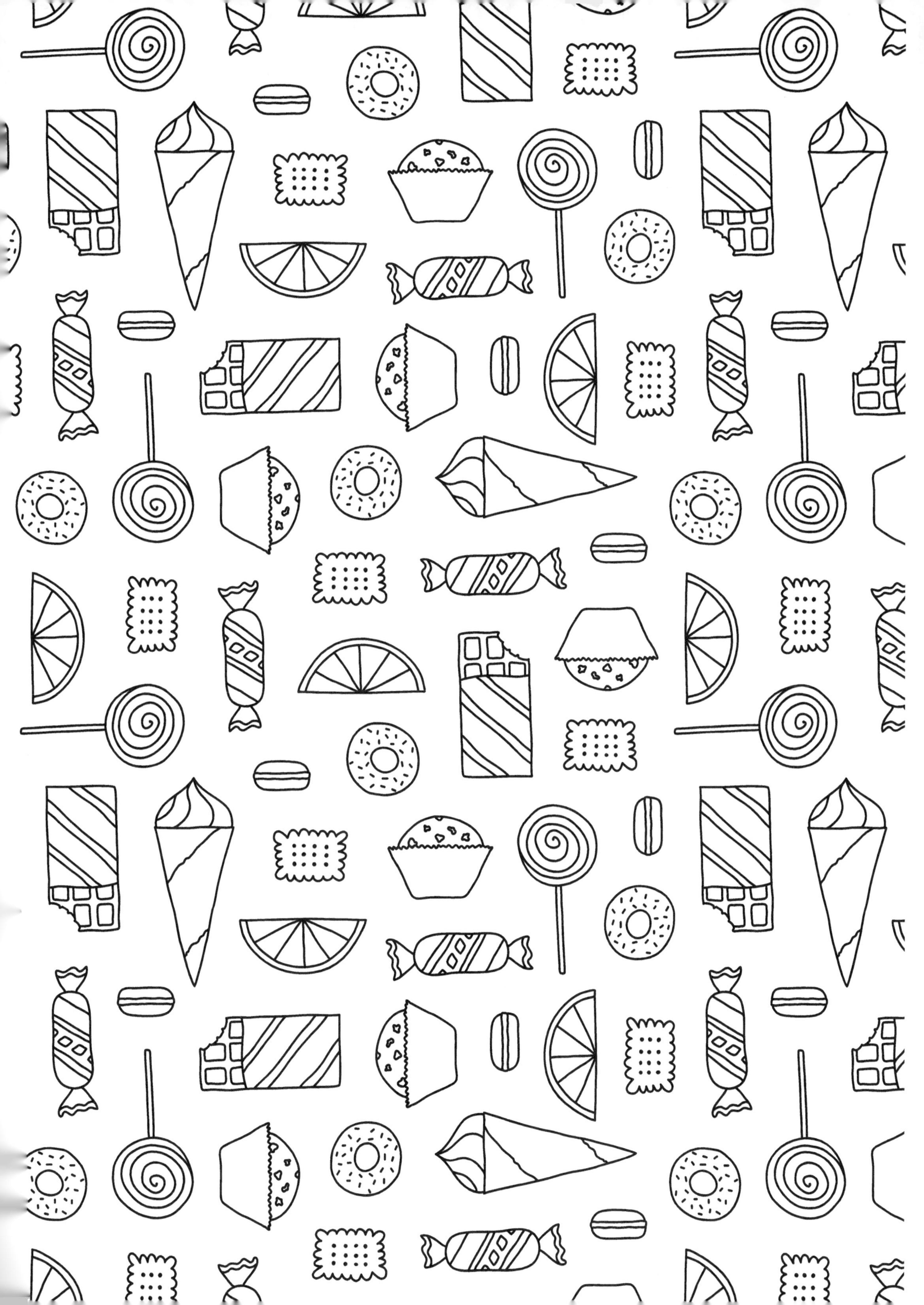

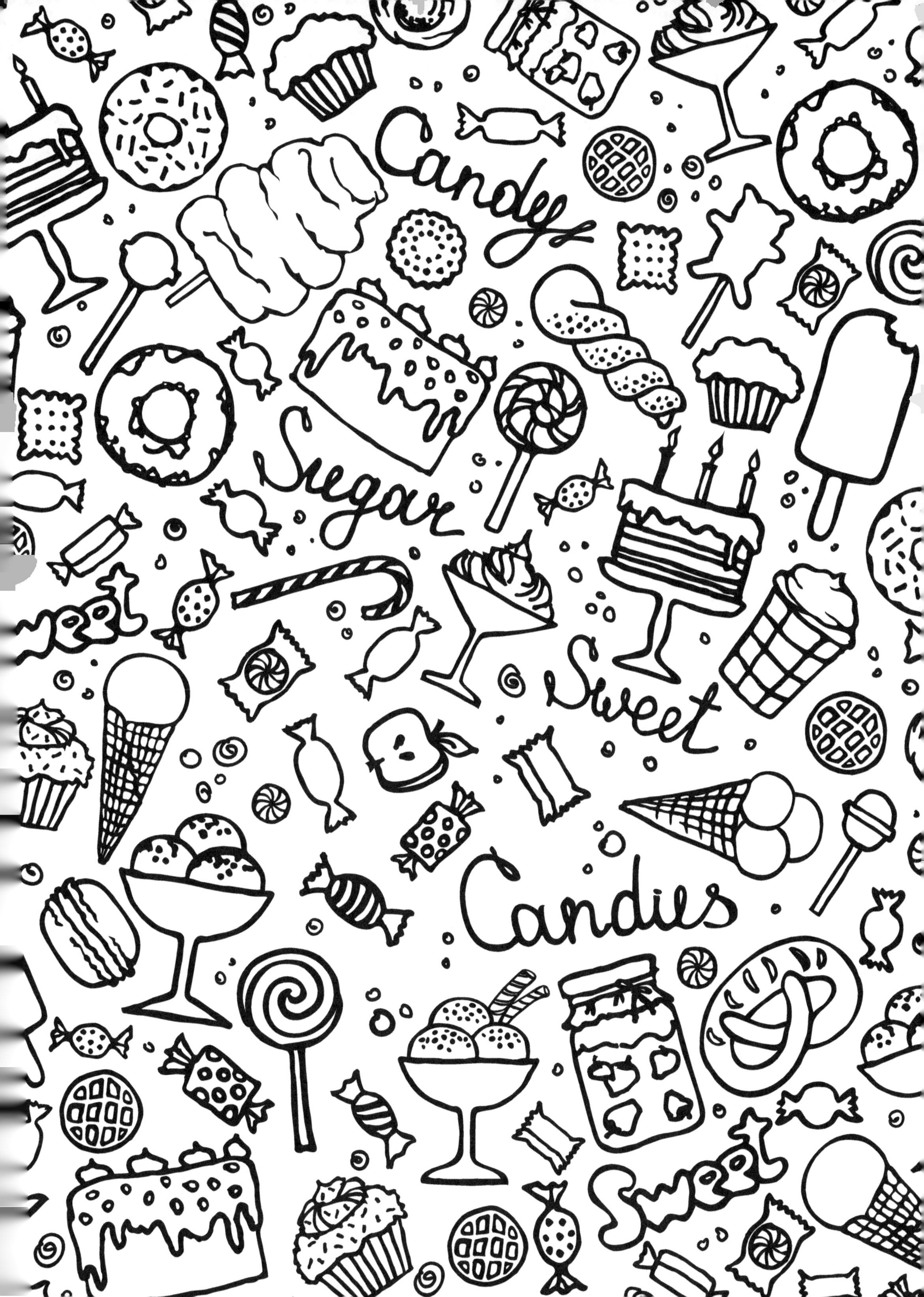

Candy
Sugar
Sweet
Candies
Sweet

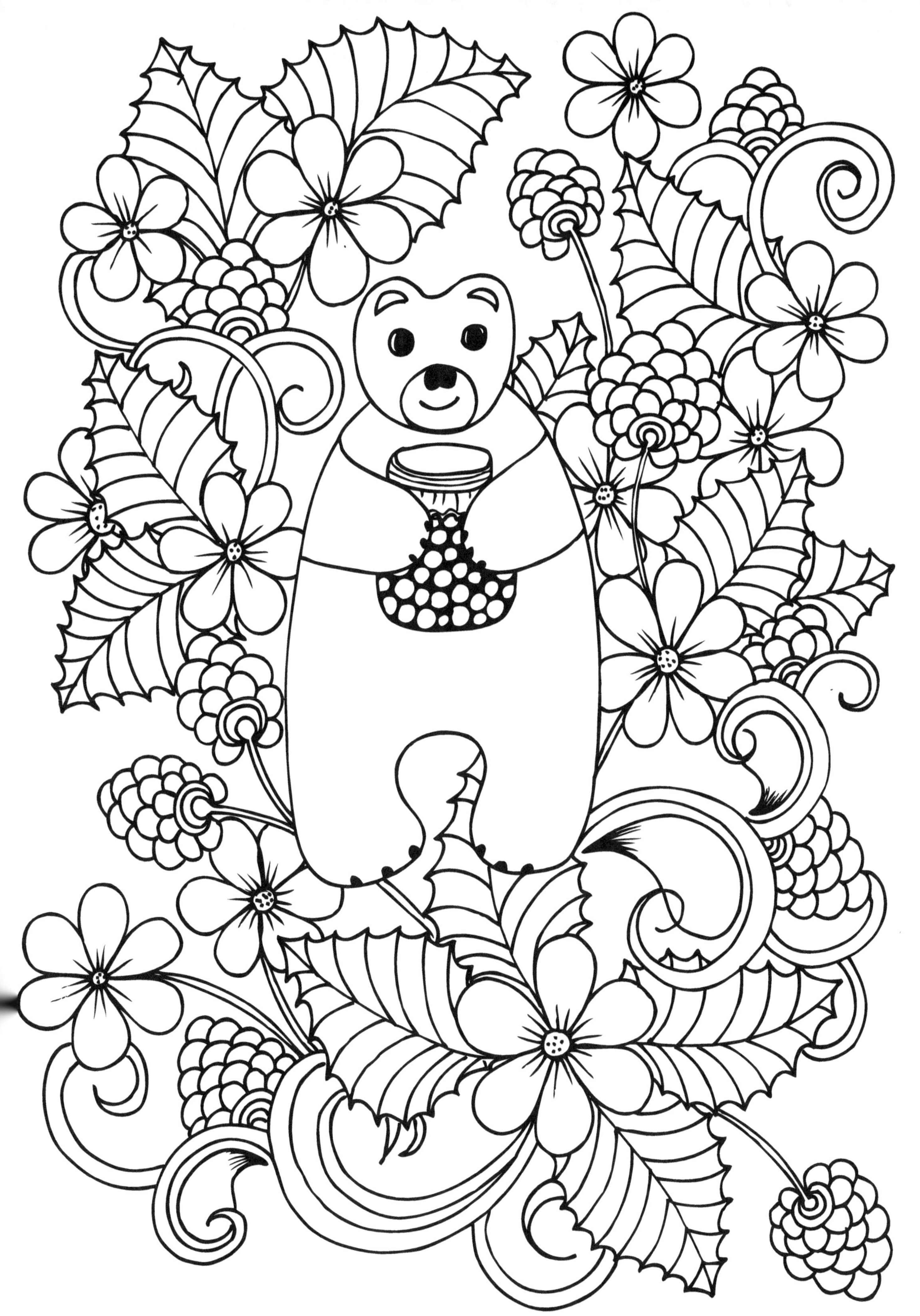

HAppy
iRthday

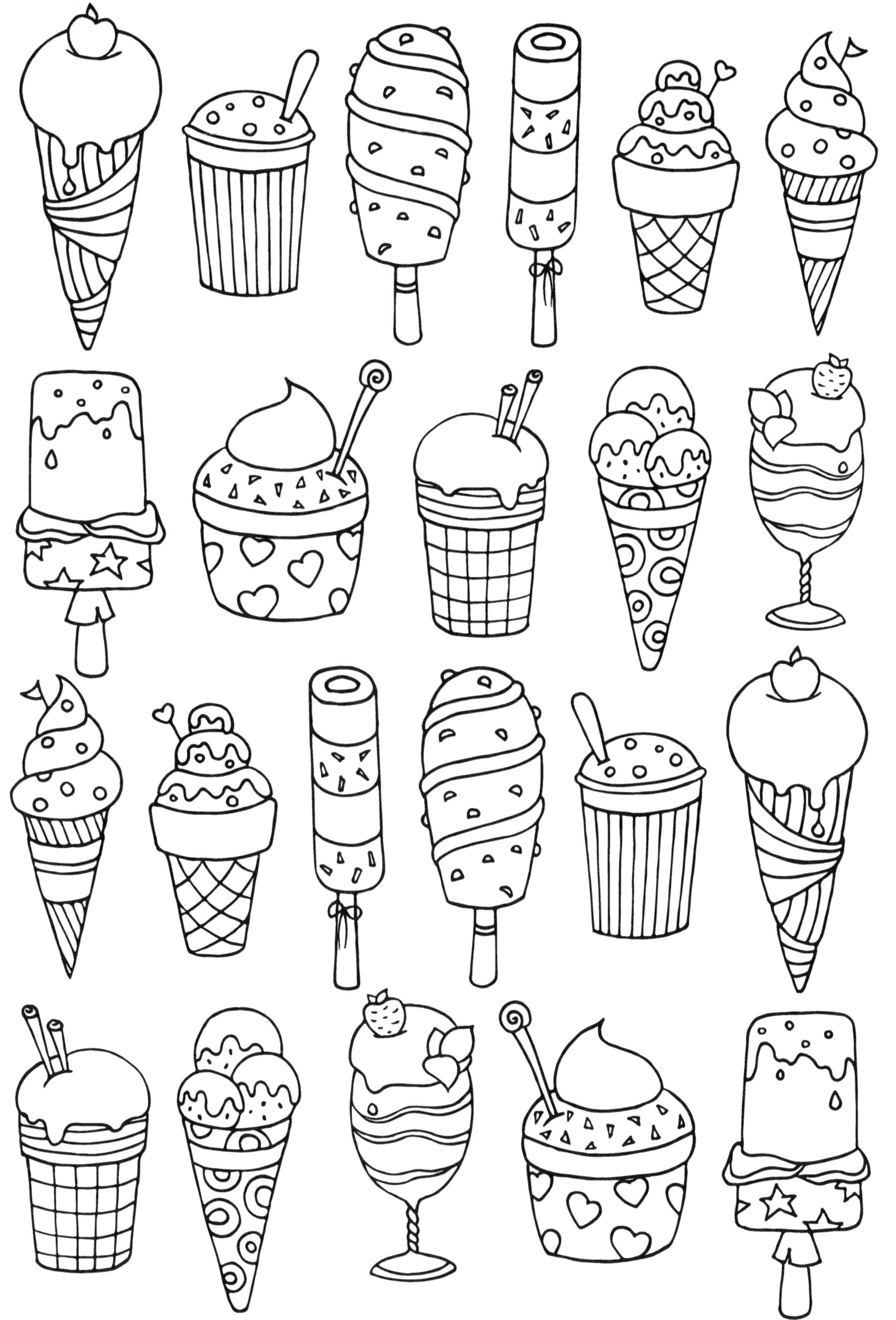

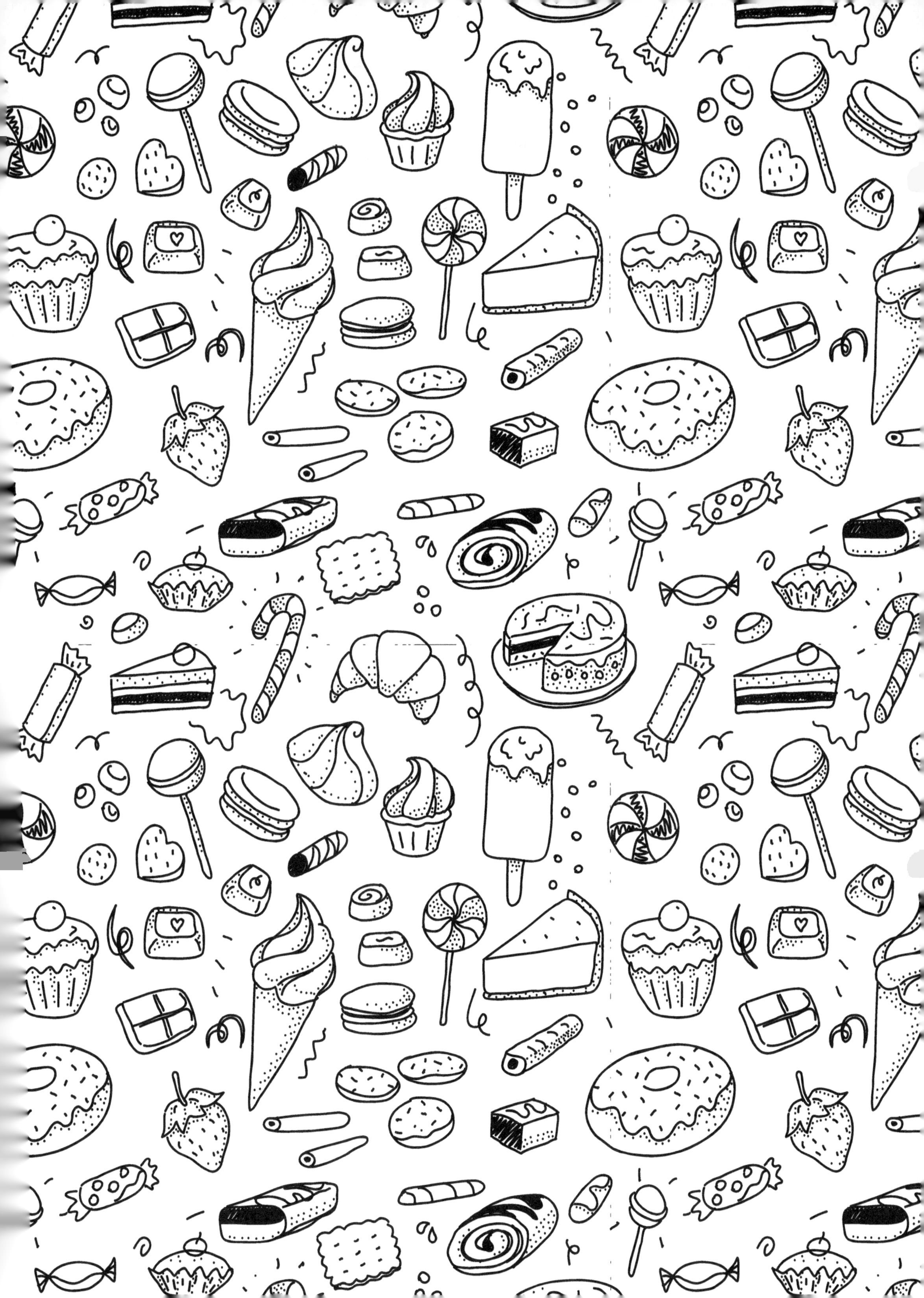

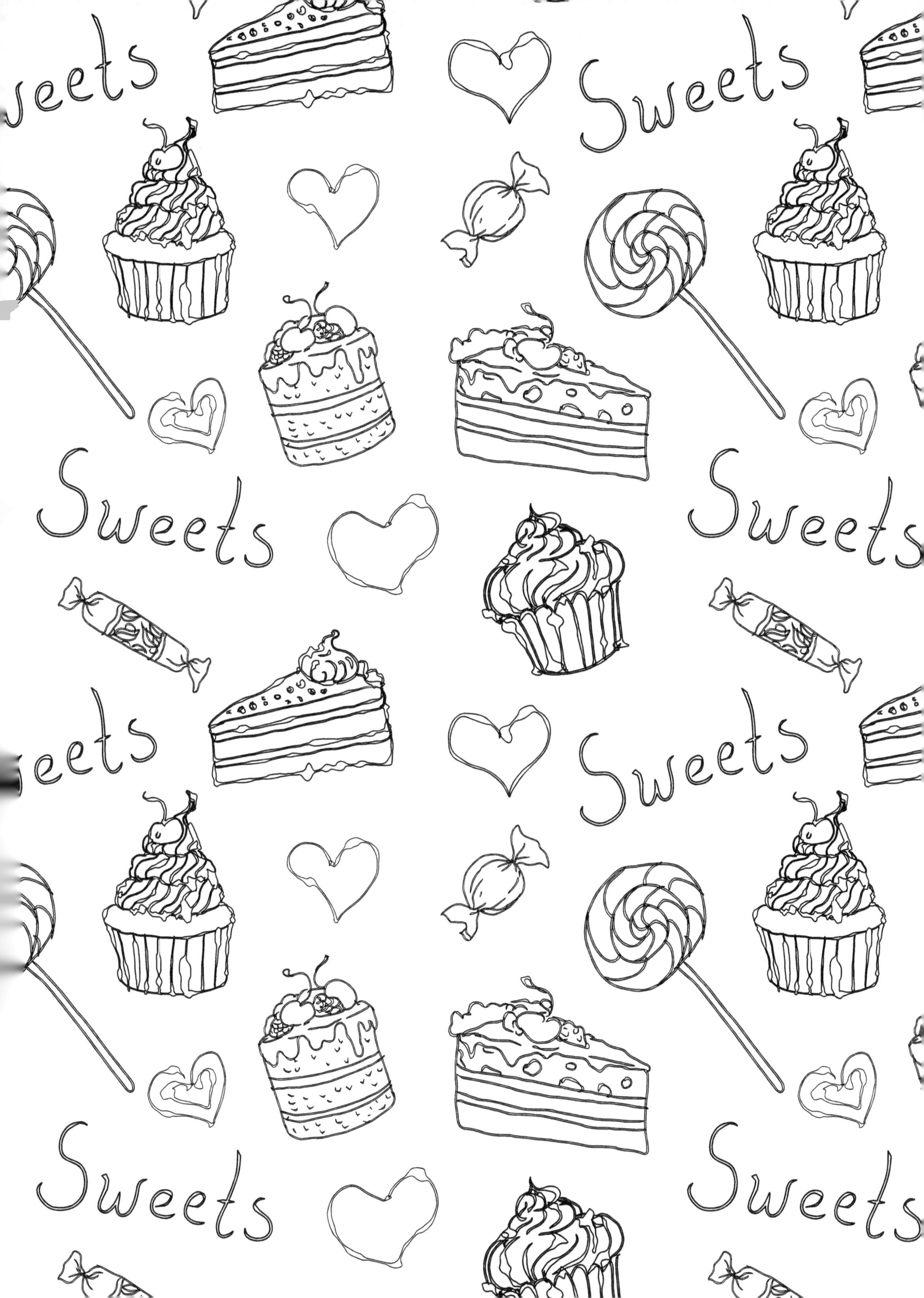
Sweets
Sweets
Sweets
Sweets
Sweets
Sweets
Sweets
Sweets

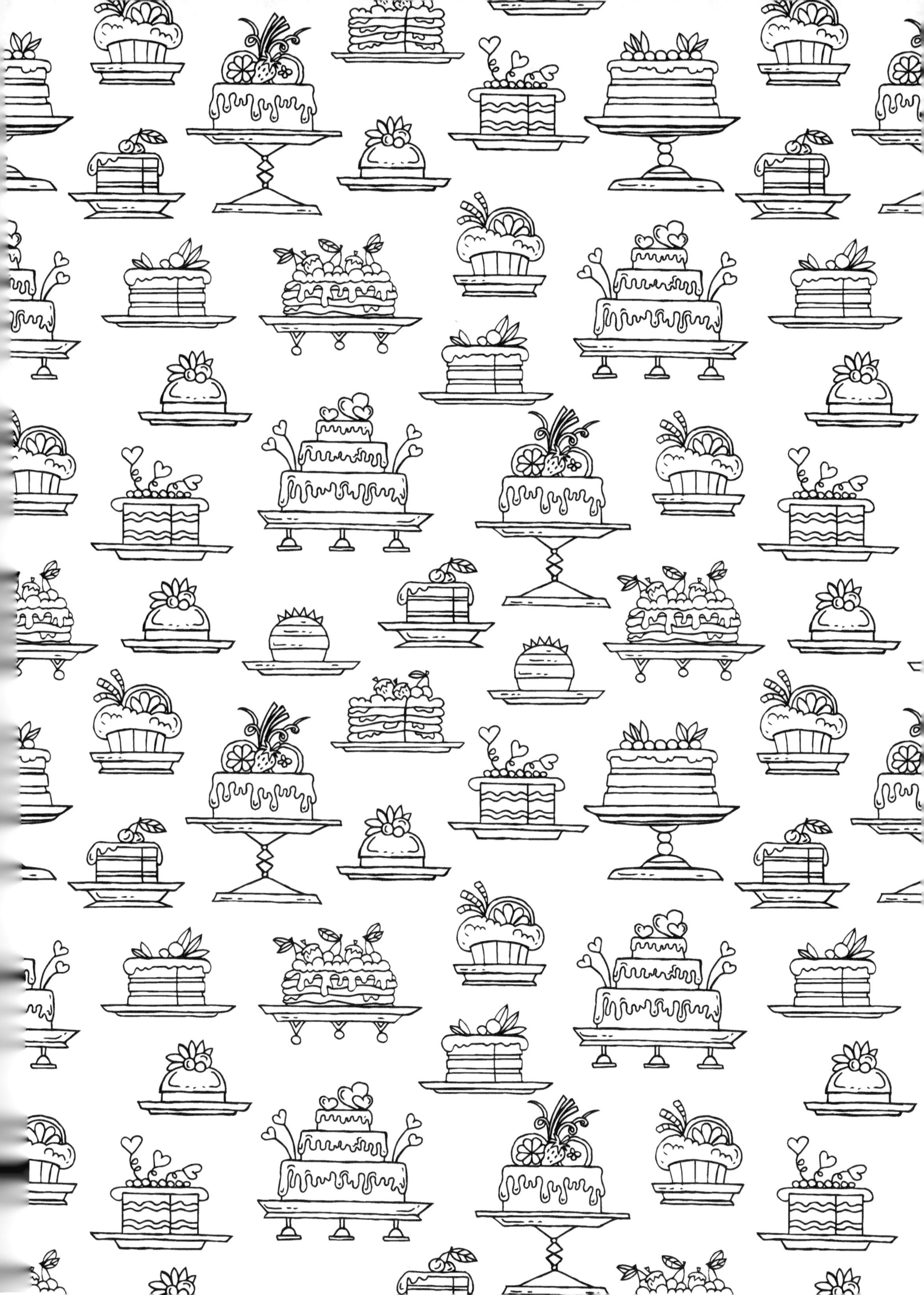

www.ingramcontent.com/pod-product-compliance
Lightning Source LLC
LaVergne TN
LVHW061255100826
845148LV00008B/1137

* 9 7 8 1 7 8 5 9 5 1 2 5 1 *